Piano for Pensioners

*The keys to playing piano
in retirement*

Kathleen Nicholson

ISBN: 9798655154513

PublishNation
www.publishnation.co.uk

Contents

Introduction

Are you too old to learn to play the piano? Many people who are over a certain age think so, but are they right?

First of all let me be clear. This is not a course of instruction in how to play the piano. So if you are looking for a book that contains some music and basic exercises, please look elsewhere. This book is intended for people who have reached retirement, find they have some spare time, and are toying with the idea of starting a new hobby.

Some people will have learnt to play the piano as a child, and perhaps have encouraged their own children through piano lessons. Others may still have the piano they used to play years ago. It stands there, a family heirloom, but apart from getting dusted, and being a good place on which to stand photographs and a vase of flowers, it is never used nowadays. Instead it gives them a guilt feeling as it is no longer used, but somehow they can't bear to part with it. It's just so frustrating to know that most of what they learnt on the piano has all but been forgotten.

Still others never had the opportunity to play the piano as a child, but they dearly wish they could play now. They see lots of adverts telling them they can learn the piano in a very short time, and wonder whether it really is possible. That is why I have decided to search for the truth, and I hope that you will find the answers you need within these pages.

For many people there is no instrument quite like the piano. Yet although lots of people started to learn when they were children, very few of those people can still play when they become adults. According to Atarah Ben-Tovim, whose pioneering work in matching children with instruments won her an award of an honorary Doctorate of Music, *'More people have been musically crippled by the piano than by all the other instruments put together'*.

That is a worrying statement, but she goes on to suggest that if you ask a few adult friends who had piano lessons as a child how much they enjoyed them, whether they still play piano today, and whether it really enriched their lives, the answers would throw up a lot of negatives.

Perhaps you were one of those who had piano lessons when you were a child. Maybe you really wanted to learn, but soon got bored with it. After all, there were so many other exciting things to fill your time. Were you in fact only continuing with lessons because your parents were keen for you to learn? Were you told that you would regret not learning how to play the piano for the rest of your life? Have you regretted never learning when you were younger, or giving up too soon? Or did you simply never have the chance to learn when you were a child, however much you may have wanted to? Only the children of wealthier families parents were not very well off so it was never an option for you.

If any of the above apply to you, be assured you are not alone. A great many adults wish they could play piano, but didn't really enjoy the lessons they had as a child. The drop out rate for young piano players is huge, and many people find that even after putting up with lessons for a few years, they can no longer read music fluently.

In fact it can take many years of lessons and practise to become a competent pianist, and one of the problems with this instrument is that you have to be pretty good at it to enable you to play with others. Those children who play a wind instrument, or a stringed instrument, in fact any instrument that requires them to follow a single notational line, will soon be able to join in a band or a school orchestra, and playing with others makes the process of learning so much more enjoyable. In contrast, playing the piano can be a lonely occupation.

Unless a child is a very rare prodigy it takes many years of lessons and practise, and also exams, to reach any degree of fluency. So a child who begins piano at age seven could reach Grade 5 or 6 by the time they are doing GCSEs. Admittedly a small number will get beyond this level, and they are quite likely to be the few who are able to play the piano as adults.

For some, schoolwork brings the perfect excuse to give it up. There simply isn't the time to practise piano when there is so much homework to be done. In any case they hadn't really been enjoying it, so what was the point of it all? They may have felt that they could never be good enough to play for or with others so in addition, it had been a lonely journey.

If it really does take a child seven or eight years to reach about Grade 5 standard, what chance is there of you now, as a retiree, ever being able to play piano well? Have you seen lots of courses advertised on line promising to get you playing piano in an unbelievably short time? Is that really possible, or is it just a scam to get you to part with your money? Because as everyone knows, children learn faster than adults, don't they? Maybe your 60+ brain will never be able cope with the intricacies of this beautiful, complex, and sometimes frustrating instrument.

If you can identify with any of these thoughts, join me on this journey to uncover the truth about learning to play the piano as an older adult.

My Own Piano Journey

First I should explain something about myself, and why I am writing this book. After all, you will want to know whether you can trust me to tell you the truth about whether it is possible to start to play the piano later in life. You may have heard that you really need to start to learn music as a young child, because like learning a new language, it is so much easier to learn when you are young.

I believe that concept is only a half truth. There is more and more evidence that the brain is able to learn new things at any time of life. Indeed, it is good to keep the brain active, and you may have read about the value of crossword puzzles, sudoku, even jigsaw puzzles. Recent research has shown that there is nothing better for exercising the brain than music. Even just listening to music has the effect of activating different parts of the brain, but playing it yourself, learning to decode all those little black dots, takes exercising the brain to a whole new level.

I am writing this having already reached and past my threescore years and ten. The piano has been a big part of the whole of my life, but only because I have had a love/hate relationship with it. In fact my mother was a piano teacher. Having taught my elder sister to play the piano it was assumed that she would teach me. My mother believed that a child under the age of seven was too young to learn the piano. I don't wholly agree with her on that although she did have a point. Up until the age of seven a child has so much to learn, including learning to read and write. I do think that for many children, whilst learning music from an even earlier age than seven is good, perhaps the piano is not the ideal instrument for them to begin on.

So I wasn't given any encouragement to play the piano before the age of seven. Indeed, I was kept away from the piano, my mother's most precious possession. She firmly believed that it was wrong to just 'mess about on the piano'. This was in line with the thinking of her day, as I am going back to the 1950's. Any attempt to play by ear was discouraged, as the belief then was that if anyone learnt to play by ear they would never learn to read music. I now think that this was quite wrong, and playing by ear is a wonderful gift to have. I have certainly known people who were very talented at playing by ear, but who were also proficient music readers as well.

When I reached the age of seven my father became seriously ill with a heart condition. My mother had to look after his market garden business until it was eventually sold, and that took quite some time. There was little money coming in, so added to health worries there were now financial worries for the family, and my mother no longer had the time nor the inclination to teach me the piano. Even if I had been allowed to 'mess around on the piano', this prized instrument was kept in the due north facing room of our fairly large house. For most of the year this room was very cold indeed. There was no central heating in the house, and no double glazed windows. The windows were often frosted over on a winter's morning, something you rarely see today. In fact there was only heat in one room in the whole house and that was the back south facing dining room, the one room in which we lived.

On just two occasions in each year a fire was lit in the front room, and these were the two times during the year when we had visitors who were invited to have tea with us. The fire was lit early morning, and had to be fed all day to keep it going, to try to raise the temperature in the room. After tea my mother would entertain the guests with playing some of her best pieces. At seven or eight years old I didn't really enjoy any of this music. All these years later I do remember them, and when I hear any of them now on the radio they bring back many memories for me. But as a young child, they certainly didn't inspire me to learn to play the piano. So after a very few random lessons, and my unwillingness to practise, my mother was glad to let my lessons go. I did remember where to find middle C on the piano, but as the years went by, very little else.

Later on during my teenage years I developed a great love of music. I had a friend who played the flute and I longed to try that, but my mother insisted that you should always learn the piano first. With the benefit of hindsight I now wonder if she said this because there was simply no money for buying an instrument, or paying for lessons on either the flute or piano. Whatever the reason it was a non starter for me. I did enjoy music lessons at secondary school, and also being part of the school choir. At that time of my life I was beginning to envy anyone who could play the piano, and from my teens and throughout my twenties I had a few failed attempts at learning to play.

Once I was working and able to fund myself I had some private lessons with a man who lived not far from us. He got very irritable over my mistakes, and one Saturday morning as I walked home in tears I suddenly asked myself why on earth was I paying for this! I didn't go back to him, but pushed a note through his door to say I didn't want any more piano lessons.

The urge to learn never left me, and in my mid twenties I signed up for a distance learning course from a place called Aldermaston College. This was a comprehensive 'teach yourself to play piano' course, which started from absolute basics right through to quite advanced music. A new lesson was sent every couple of weeks, and it built up into a file of 96 lessons. I still have the complete set of lessons, and I did make some progress with it. By this time my father had died, having been an invalid for thirteen years, and my mother had again started taking in a few piano pupils. She did show some interest in the course and was able to give me a little help, although her teaching style was rather too much like the man who I had gone to for paid lessons, and it didn't make for good relationships at home. Whilst the early lessons of this course were helpful they soon became much too difficult for me, so although I continued to collect each part, I gave up attempting the lessons which were way beyond my skill level.

At the age of thirty I moved away from my home town and bought a small house. For some reason I wanted a piano, and managed to acquire one which had been in an old church hall. It wasn't in good condition but had once been a fine piano, and a piano tuner that I consulted for advice thought he could bring it up to an acceptable standard for me. When I got it, it was full of pigeon feathers, and an old mouse's nest! A good clean with a vacuum cleaner, and a couple of tunings transformed it, and it came to my new house. At last I was able to fiddle around on it and amuse myself. But although I enjoyed the few things that I could play in my own way, I never made any real progress. Sadly it seemed that I just didn't have what it took to become a pianist.

That old piano came with me when I got married, because, even though I couldn't really play it, I did love it. It was the first piano my little daughter played. Even in pre school years she often went to it, and enjoyed the sounds it made. She showed some musical promise from a very young age, and I believe my mother's talent skipped a generation with me and was passed down to my daughter, who later became a professional music teacher. When my mother died we exchanged the old piano and bought a new one for our then fourteen year old daughter. This became another much loved piano.

I have told you about my piano journey so that you will see that by the time I retired at the age of 62 I really could hardly play the piano at all. The longing was still there though. I now had time to spare, and also a little money to fund a new hobby. Was it possible to become a pianist at my age? I was determined to find out.

My daughter married when I was 60 and of course she needed to take her piano with her to her new home. Could I survive without a piano in the house? In fact I didn't have to as the family bought me a little digital piano to celebrate my 60 years. It was about this time that our son, who was obviously musical but had never been interested in learning piano the traditional way, showed me a way of playing the piano which was far easier than any method I had known before.

I shall explain this in more detail later on. For now, I just want to make the point that if you have ever played the piano as a child, and passed a couple of grade exams, but then not touched a piano for years you are in fact further on than I was when I retired. But even if you don't know how to find middle C on a piano there is still hope. All you need is the desire to play, the will to explore every aspect of this wonderful instrument, and importantly the determination to practise. You can do it!

Understanding Your Reasons

If you feel you would like to play the piano, but wonder whether you have any chance at all of learning later in life, you must understand that your success depends on a number of important factors. So before going any further I would urge you to examine your reasons for wanting to play the piano, because these reasons could determine the course of learning which you decide to take.

You will appreciate that there are many different styles of music, and not everyone likes all these different styles. In fact most of us have our distinct preferences, and what is music to the ears of some people is just a racket to others. So it's worth thinking about the different types of music you would like to learn to play, as this could help to determine the course you choose to take, or the sort of teacher you need.

Almost all children who learn the piano from a professional teacher will learn by what is called the classical method. This is good, and should give them an all round education in music, enabling them to adopt any style as they progress. If they start at age seven, and they stick at it, they may then have ten years in which to progress to become a good pianist. Unfortunately some children become disheartened by this method, bored with some of the music they have to learn for exams, put off by parents nagging them to practise when they would much rather be doing something more sociable, and finding the pressures of school work making it impossible to continue.

Ten years can seem a long time, but if you, wanting to start piano in retirement, can imagine yourself being a competent all round pianist in ten years from now, then go ahead and take this classical route. There is no reason at all why you shouldn't also make the grade, just because you are beginning at a later age.

In fact you may well learn faster than a child because it is something that you really want to do, and you will be free of some of the social and educational pressures that sometimes get in the way of children's musical learning. For some children, possibly many, practising the piano is just another chore, something that they have to do like the rest of their homework, and the sooner they get it over with the better. But in retirement you will find that your time at the piano is a joy, and the time just flies by. You decide you have just twenty minutes to practise, but before you know it forty five minutes have gone! So because it's something you really want to do, given the right instruction you may well reach your goal in less than ten years.

Here is why thinking about and deciding upon what you really want to get from piano playing is so important. Do you want to be a concert pianist? Well, we're told 'never say never', but I have to admit I think it quite unlikely that you will achieve that if you only start at 60 plus. But that doesn't mean you can't learn to play the piano well for your own enjoyment, and for the pleasure of others.

Do you love classical music? Are you a fan of Chopin, Mozart or Beethoven? Playing some of the works of the great masters is definitely achievable, even starting later in life. But some people who may enjoy listening to this sort of music don't necessarily want to play it themselves. There are those who would just like to be able to play a few carols at Christmas, or nursery rhymes for their grandchildren. If you can identify with this I can promise you that you can do this in a much shorter time than ten years!

Some people reading this will have their hearts set on playing jazz. It is highly likely that any traditional course will touch on playing jazz at some point. Sometimes known as America's most popular export, jazz began as the blues in New Orleans around 1900. There are those who say that jazz must always be improvised spontaneously, and made up as the player goes along. If they are right, then it makes jazz very difficult to teach. Having said that, we know that lots of jazz has been committed to paper. Think of George Gershwin's 'Rhapsody in Blue' for a good example.

It must be admitted though that jazz can be very divisive, in that many people either love it or hate it. It is included in most courses of study today because whether you are a fan of jazz or not it is good to be familiar with all types of music. It seems to me also that those who love jazz have a natural understanding of it, and it is lack of that understanding that makes others hate it. So if you love jazz and long to play it then go for it, and find a teacher who will allow you to focus on it. You will always learn more easily the music you love.

Those who learn by what is known as the chord piano route are bound to meet the Blues, because it is such a big influence on popular music. Chord progressions are the building blocks of this method. In it's simplest form you would be using just three chords. If you learn only three chords for whatever key you want to play in you can have hours of fun experimenting with lots of popular tunes.

So three of the keys to learning to play the piano in retirement are to find the right course of study, the right teaching/learning method to help you achieve being able play the music you hope to play, and also a teacher who can help you follow your dreams. Of these three, the teacher could be the most important of all. In fact, do you need an actual teacher at all, or could you teach yourself?

My feelings about teachers are they can make or break the dream for you. By all means look for a teacher if you feel you cannot make progress without one. But as an adult don't forget that you are in control. You will be paying for a teacher's services, and you must get value for money. Look out for all the teachers who advertise in the local press or on the internet, but also listen to recommendations from others. Do you know of anyone who is learning with a particular teacher? Is that person getting on well, and is satisfied with the progress he or she is making?

Try to book a trial lesson with any teacher that you find, and shop around. This will give you some idea of each person's teaching style. Is the teacher someone you can get on well with? We all find some people easier to get on with than others, and if you are going to enjoy your piano lessons it is essential that you have a good, adult relationship with the person who is teaching.

Be aware that the majority of piano teachers will follow the traditional route of teaching you to play the piano, but there are teachers who accept that there are other ways for adults to learn. So if it's just popular songs you really want to play you might be able to find a teacher who will show you a simpler method. In fact some people believe that the rules and techniques of classical piano are not appropriate for playing non-classical music.

So at your trial lesson be sure to make very clear to the teacher what your aims are. Does the teacher use only one method, and has he/she got any experience with teaching adults? This is essential, as a very different approach is needed when teaching adults rather than children. What sort of music do they suggest that you start with? If you are a complete beginner, do they recommend a tutor book that is aimed at adults rather than children? You will soon become disillusioned if you only play from books geared at children, and don't quickly get beyond 'Mary had a little lamb' and 'Row row row the boat'.

Do you need a lesson every week? A child probably does, and lessons are usually for half an hour once a week. Adults may well fare better with lessons that are longer than that, but they may not need to go every week. Is the teacher flexible enough to allow fortnightly lessons, or even once a month if that's what suits you? I'm sure you understand yourself well enough to know which style of learning is best for you. We all learn in different ways, and some people need the pressure of a weekly lesson to keep them focused. But some adults find weekly lessons too stressful, and because they are enjoying being at their piano and so are loving their practise times, one lesson every two or three weeks might actually be more effective for them. Also, for some people, weekly lessons may be simply too costly.

Perhaps you are thinking about teaching yourself the piano. If you search the internet you will find many adverts telling you that you can learn to play the piano in almost no time at all. Should you believe them? Can you really learn in just a few weeks? Can you actually learn online?

Let me take you back to thinking about your reasons for learning, and what you really want to achieve. If you are one of those who say they really wish they could play the piano but are not wanting to play some great works of complicated classical music, but rather just wish they could play some simple songs, there has never been a better time than now to do this, as modern technology has brought the dream within your grasp.

So to answer some of those questions above, yes, if you really want to be able to play some classical music in it's original form, or if you are a jazz enthusiast, you almost certainly do need the guidance of a competent teacher. But if you want to play some popular songs, or hymns or Christmas carols, there are simpler methods to reach your goals, and whilst you do need some instruction there are some very good courses online which can help you to get started putting melodies and chords together just for the fun of it.

Can you learn to play the piano in just three weeks? One advert I saw recently made that claim, but as I have already stated, my answer is no you can't. That promise is misleading. I assume the advert is simply referring to a course which just shows you how to get started, but while you may be delighted with yourself for being able to play a simple melody with three chords in a very short time you will hardly be able to call yourself a pianist in three weeks. But if you have good instruction, online or with a teacher, you will certainly be able to play some of your favourite songs reasonably well in just a few months. And for however long you learn, by which ever method you choose to take, there is always more to to be grasped, always something to be improved upon, always some new delight just around the corner. That is the joy of learning to play the piano.

What sort of instrument
do you need?

If you want to learn to play the piano it is essential that you have at least some sort of keyboard instrument in your own home. You may be surprised to learn that not everyone understands that, but the truth is without an instrument at home to practise on you will not get very far.

What sort of instrument you will be learning on depends upon what you may have already, and what your intentions are. For example, are you just wanting to dip your toes in to see if this is for you, or are you going to seriously pursue becoming a pianist? It also depends on how much space you have in your home, how close you are to neighbours, how willing other family members are for you to learn to play, even what your gut feeling tells you about what sort of instrument would be right for you. Also let's not forget your budget. It could cost you anything from nothing at all, if you're lucky enough to have someone who wants to give you one, or tens of thousands of pounds for the best grand piano you can buy! For most people it will be somewhere in between those two extremes.

So what options do you have? Let's look for a moment at those who have no instrument at home already, but just feel they want to try out learning to play piano. Do they need a real acoustic piano, or would a smaller, cheaper electronic keyboard do just as well?

It needs to be pointed out that those smaller electronic keyboards may look similar to a piano, but they are in fact a different instrument altogether. In the same way, a clavichord, a spinnet, or even an organ are all keyboard instruments, but they are all different. The layout of the keys may be the same, but the feel of them will be unique to each instrument.

There is no doubt that electronic keyboards have brought music within reach of many people who previously would never have attempted to play an instrument. They are relatively cheap to buy, and they have lots of features that do some of the work for you. For instance, they come with an assortment of backing tracks which fill out the music for you, providing harmony for the melodies you play, sometimes with a single notational line in the right hand and using one finger for chords in the left hand. They do have their place for people who just want to enjoy themselves with some popular music, but they have their limitations. Many people who learn to play the electronic keyboard find that before too long they become bored with the same old tracks. They are not able to play very much music written specifically for the keyboard on an ordinary piano because with no backing tracks it feels empty, and in any case the feel of the keys on a real piano is not the same as they have become accustomed to.

The 'feel' of the keys, or the 'weight' of the keys is all important when transferring from one instrument to another, because pressing the keys down on an electronic keyboard is so different from the feel of acoustic piano keys. So if it's the piano you really want to learn it would be preferable not to start on one of these electronic keyboard instruments. However, if space and budget are an issue, or if someone is offering you one for free, they do all come with a 'piano' button which will give you a fairly realistic sound. The black and white keys will be laid out in the same fashion, and even though there will not be as many there are enough to get you started. If you do get a keyboard make sure you get a pedal which can be attached to it, and try to get the best one you can afford. Every keyboard will have a socket at the back of it for introducing a pedal, and it will make a difference to your playing even though you may not have needed one when using the electronic sounds that you have got used to.

Some people get confused with the difference between electronic keyboards and digital pianos. However there is considerable difference between the two, even though some may look quite similar. The first thing you may notice, if you go into a shop which sells both electronic keyboards and digital pianos, is that the digital pianos almost all have 88 keys. You needn't try to count them, but you will realise that they are the same length as an acoustic piano, which almost always has 88 keys. There are a few digital pianos which have 76 keys, and if space is a problem for you one of these may be acceptable at the beginning of your musical journey, but if possible, if it's the piano you want to learn to play, do try to get 88 keys.

With some of these digital pianos you will also have to buy a stand on which to put it. These pianos are very portable, and can even be hidden away, for example underneath a bed or settee when not in use, but be sure to put a cover over it if you do this, or dust will soon become a problem. Again, if you acquire one of these pianos make sure you buy the best pedal you can afford to go with it.

For the home there are many more digital pianos which vary considerably in size, but come with wooden surrounds to fit in with any other furnishings you may have. Even though they almost all will have 88 keys the size of them will vary considerably, so be sure to measure up how much room you have before you buy one. These pianos will usually have at least two pedals integral to the body of the piano, and most now have three. In your early months of learning you will only actually use one.

A digital piano is of course an electronic instrument, and so needs to be plugged in and switched on. It has the advantage of a volume control, and you can also use it with headphones which is ideal if you want to play without disturbing others, as with the headphones on only you yourself will be able to hear the piano.

Digital pianos vary considerably in price, from a few hundred pounds to a few thousand pounds for one that looks like a grand piano. In recent years the trend has been for the woodwork to be built looking more and more like an acoustic piano, and on some, where the key cover hides the controls it can be hard to immediately see the difference. If you decide to go for a digital piano it is wise to choose a well known make. See Appendix 2 for some suggestions. Also if at all possible take someone who is a pianist with you when you buy one, because once again the feel of the keys, and how weighted they are, is all important in getting you off to a good start.

When they were first on the market there was a lot of criticism of digital pianos, but I believe over the years they have been vastly improved, and some of the best ones are very good indeed. Are they the same as an acoustic piano? The honest answer is no. An acoustic piano is a very special instrument and it can provide you with a response that a digital piano, which is basically something artificial, can never give you. In spite of that it has to be said that a good digital piano is a far better option than a bad acoustic piano – and there are some bad ones around.

Some advantages of a digital piano, besides the ones mentioned above are that they are much more easily moved, if you find it necessary, for example to move it to another room. They are almost always extremely reliable, and perhaps the biggest plus of all is that they never go out of tune, and so never need tuning. In these days of centrally heated homes this can be a huge factor, and as some acoustic pianos need tuning a couple of times a year it is worth taking this into account, as piano tuning is not cheap.

Digital pianos, like electronic keyboards, also have the option of producing sounds other than piano sounds on them. This may or may not appeal to you. If it's just a piano you want to learn make sure you tell any sales people this. There is no point paying for all the extra sounds that may be on offer if you feel you will never use them. One useful option however is the ability to record yourself playing, so make sure that the instrument you go for can do this.

There will be an instrument to suit all budgets, so do shop around. You may also be able to get a very good deal second hand. Buying on eBay could be risky, especially if it's from a private seller where there is no chance of returning it. But some piano dealers sometimes have second hand digital pianos in stock which have been traded in when a customer has upgraded to an acoustic piano. There are some very good deals to be had with these, and the seller will have checked the instrument over before selling it on, so you should be able to get a guarantee with it.

We have now arrived at a discussion on acoustic pianos. There is no doubt that these should be the best, but as mentioned above, a good digital piano is far better than a poor acoustic. There have often been pianos advertised saying 'suitable for a beginner'. What does that actually mean? If you see those words in a private advert be very cautious indeed, because it often means that some of the notes don't play or they have a poor tone. Pianos, unless they are the very finest makes and have always been well maintained, do not last for ever, and a piano that has been neglected and unloved for years is unlikely to be a good option for a beginner.

It is absolutely essential that your first instrument is in tune, and has no faulty notes, because if it doesn't sound good you will soon become disillusioned with your piano playing and probably give it up altogether. Pianos really do need to be tuned at least once a year. Without this they will drop in pitch, especially if they are kept in a centrally heated home, and once the pitch drops a single tuning may not be enough to bring it up to a good standard. Older pianos in particular have suffered from centrally heated homes, because lots of them were made before central heating became standard. A cold room is usually better for the piano, though not for the pianist!

More recently the materials used in making pianos have been given special treatment enabling them to withstand the warmer temperature better. Even so some pianos will still do better if they are fitted with a dehumidifier, though they can be expensive. Failing that there is an old trick of removing the lower front panel of the piano and standing half a cup of water inside, then replacing the panel. This often seems to help if you have a piano with any keys that stick, but do ask your piano tuner for advice about it first.

If you do come across an older piano that someone wants to be rid of, try to take a pianist with you to test it out before agreeing to purchase it. You will also have to factor in the cost of transporting the piano to your home. Be very careful before you agree to letting friends, who may have access to a suitable van, move the piano for you. Most people who are not experienced with acoustic pianos are completely unaware just how heavy they are, and how difficult they are to move without the right equipment. Pianos are built with an iron frame inside, and considerable damage can be done to a piano being handled in the wrong way by well meaning people, to say nothing of injury to the human's frame. Professional piano moving can be costly, but if the piano is any good at all it is worth moving it correctly to avoid damage.

Suppose you already have a piano in your home, but it hasn't been used or tuned for years, what should you do? It is probably best if you seek the advice of a good piano tuner, to see whether it is worth tuning once or twice to bring it up to standard. Some old pianos will be full of dust and debris, and the felts may have been attacked by moths. A tuner will be able to examine it for you and thoroughly clean it out, replacing any worn felts or broken strings. Or you may be advised that it simply isn't worth the expense and that you are better starting afresh. Actually I understand that there are very few pianos which are completely beyond repair and refurbishment, but you may need to balance out the cost with buying a new, or new to you second hand piano, as this may be the better option. This is sad if you are very attached to your piano, which may seem like an old friend to you, but it is better to know the truth from the start.

Disposing of an old worn out piano can be difficult. Piano dealers are in the main not interested in any piano that is over twenty years old, unless it is one of the elite German pianos, such as a Bechstein or a Bosendorfer. Also I'm sure every one has heard of the Steinway piano. Henry E. Steinway himself was in fact a German immigrant to America, originally called Heinrich Engelhard Steinweg (1797 – 1871). He used his German expertise when creating the Steinway piano, and these are usually considered to be among the very best. More recently Yamaha pianos have also become highly thought of, and they usually keep their value well.

If you do want to exchange your otherwise ordinary piano for a more modern one it is worth consulting various piano dealers throughout the country. There are some dealers who will literally only take pianos of specific makes, whilst there are a few others who will take just about anything they can get. Some of these dealers will strip down old pianos, taking out anything they consider recyclable, and then sometimes selling the woodwork, perhaps on eBay both in the UK and also in America where there seems to be a market for old cabinets.

You will probably not be given much for an old poor piano, but sometimes it is just worth having someone take it away for you. Sadly some will simply be broken up for firewood.

Many dealers, who sell new pianos, will also have a reasonable selection of second hand pianos, often instruments which have been traded in when someone has upgraded. Buying a second hand from a trusted dealer should be a good option as the piano will have been examined carefully, tuned and repaired before resale, and should definitely come with a warranty. Some dealers will have pianos listed as 'beginner' pianos, but you can be sure that what a good dealer sells you will be in proper working order. It could be that these pianos are not a particularly well known make and therefore will not hold their value as well as a more expensive piano. Nevertheless such a piano could serve you well for a long time to come, providing it is well looked after and given regular tunings.

Acoustic pianos are quite individual instruments, and whether you are buying new or second hand, if at all possible try to listen to the sound of a few before you decide on the one you want. The tone of the piano you get is all important, and not everyone likes the same sound. Do you want a bright tone, or would you prefer something more mellow? At this stage you may not know the answer to this, but so long as the tone is pleasing to you, you will enjoy your time with it and be encouraged to play it.

Should you get an upright piano, or a grand piano? Of course the answer to this may be determined by both space in your home, and finance. If you have the room, and can afford it, a grand piano, or even a baby grand, is a wonderful instrument. Most people will not have room in their home for such a large piano and so will settle for an upright.

Almost all pianos made in the last twenty years will be called 'overstrung' pianos. This means that the inside of the piano can be likened to a harp on it's side. Some older pianos were simply 'vertical' and therefore had shorter strings inside them. Overstrung pianos have longer strings and this has a very positive effect on the tone of the piano, so much so that very few pianos with shorter strings are made today. Upright (vertical) pianos were for obvious reasons a cheaper option. It is worth asking a dealer about any piano you are interested in whether it is overstrung. Grand pianos, even baby grands, of course have even longer strings which in turn enhances the tone of the piano and also increases the volume. Concert grand pianos are huge, often about 9ft in length, and they contain very long strings, and have a big volume. You would not want one of these in your home!

In recent years there is one further option to consider when buying a piano. The hybrid piano is now available, and these give the authentic feel of an acoustic piano, but they also have a built in switch which converts them to digital. The advantage of this is that you get the satisfactory playing experience of acoustic, but if you need to play quietly, or even with headphones, you can do so at the touch of a button. You can even record yourself with ease. These pianos will probably become the instrument of choice for the future, though at the time of writing this they are expensive.

Pros and Cons of
Acoustic and Digital Pianos

Just to recap in brief what we've been discussing, here are the pros and cons of acoustic pianos and digital pianos. Weigh these up, as they may help you to decide which instrument best suits your needs.

Acoustic Pianos – pros

1) They are a better investment, in money and also in your future if you are serious about becoming a pianist. If you ever get beyond Grade 5 or 6, you will almost certainly need an acoustic piano by then.
2) The sound of a good piano cannot really be matched by any electronic instrument.
3) You get more feedback from an acoustic piano – all the many moving parts respond as you play and so they are more sensitive to any feelings you put into your playing.
4) They are often a beautiful piece of furniture.

Cons
1) They can be expensive to buy.
2) They take up a lot of room.
3) They are very heavy, so difficult to move without proper equipment.

4) They need tuning at least once every year, sometimes more. Some pianos hold their tune better than others. Some are affected by the humidity of the room, especially if they are kept in a warm atmosphere.

Digital pianos - pros

1) They are less expensive to buy, unless you are considering top of the range.
You can usually find a digital piano to suit most pockets.
2) The quality in recent years has vastly improved and many people find it difficult to tell the difference between digital and acoustic. (However, an experienced pianist will just *know.)*
3) There are sizes that will fit into any home. Some for a table top, others with their own stand, and yet others that are in a wooden cabinet and so are a little more permanent and part of the furniture.
4) They are very portable. Even the ones in a wooden cabinet are easier to move than an acoustic piano, and no special equipment is needed.
5) They never need tuning, so there is no ongoing expense of having the piano tuned.
6) They are not affected by changes in atmospheric pressure.
7) They very rarely go wrong, but will give good service for years.

Cons
1) Technology moves so fast that they will not hold their price.
2) After the first year's warranty finding someone to repair a digital piano can be very difficult. Sales people are far more interested in selling you a new piano.
3) The quality of digital pianos does vary, and not all will have weighted keys. Some will feel better than others, and it is important to go for a well known trusted make, and not just the cheapest.
4) You need a source of electricity as they have to be plugged in somewhere.

The bottom line is that while an acoustic piano is by far the superior instrument, a good digital is much better for a beginner than a poor acoustic – and as has been said before, there are a lot of neglected pianos out there. Ultimately the choice is yours.

You need to keep a dust cover over the keys of your piano, whatever sort you have. If it is a cheaper, portable digital piano it should come with a fabric or plastic key cover, so be sure to use it. On more expensive digital pianos slide the key cover in place when you have finished playing, and in the same way close the lid on any acoustic piano. Failing to do this means that dust will get inside and between the keys, and over a period of time this will build up and may start to cause problems.

It used to be thought that keeping the piano lid down made the keys turn yellow. This may have been the case a long time ago when piano keys were made of ivory. That does not apply these days as ivory keys, sometimes known as having come from an elephant's grave yard, are at last thankfully highly illegal. Manufacturers now use other materials for their keys and these will not turn yellow when covered.

The only other care needed is to occasionally wipe the keys with a slightly damp cloth, although be very careful not to get water in the mechanism. Apart from that just dust the top of the piano regularly.

It is not wise to put too much on top of the piano, and certainly not a vase of flowers, or a coffee cup. If these were to tip over it could spell disaster for your precious instrument. Think carefully before putting too many framed photographs on your piano. Sometimes they can vibrate when you play causing an annoying rattle. It is better, as far as you are able to put as little as possible on the top of the piano.

What else do you need to consider?

Once you have got a piano that you like you need a piano stool. If you are buying a new piano, either acoustic or digital, it is quite likely that you will be offered a matching stool to go with it. The important thing is that whatever you sit on needs to be a comfortable height for yourself. Some piano stools are adjustable so if you can get one like this you should be able to achieve the perfect height for playing your piano.

If you are getting a portable digital piano you will also need to get a pedal, which will fit into the back of the piano with a jack pin. Be sure to get the best one that you can afford, preferably one that looks as much like an ordinary piano pedal as possible, as these are far easier to use and more stable than the cheaper ones that look like a small square box.

All other pianos, upright acoustic, grand pianos or less portable digital pianos will have at least two pedals, and many will have three. If you are just starting to play the piano you will only need to understand one pedal, and that is the one on the right, which you naturally operate with your right foot.

This is known as the damper pedal, because when you press it down with your foot it holds back the dampers that quiet the strings after you release the keys your fingers are playing. Without the dampers the strings would continue to reverberate as you move on to play other notes, causing a discordant sound.

But sometimes you want the notes to continue to sound, so used correctly, it makes everything sound better, smoother and more professional. This is the case for most pieces of music, although for some music, or some parts of some music, you want the effect to be the opposite of smooth. However smooth playing, known as legato, is more common. Piano teachers will try to help you to achieve this smooth legato playing without using the pedal, and that is a good skill to have, but you will nevertheless want to learn the correct way of using this pedal to get the most artistic result. Most music will give you some indication as to where to use the pedal, although with practise and experience you will develop a natural and automatic sense of when to depress the pedal.

However do take care not to overuse the pedal, thereby causing too rich a mixture and discords. Use it sparingly to blend tones together and to sustain tones, but always release the pedal when the harmony changes. Remember - it can magnify mistakes too!

On a modern grand piano, and some upright pianos with three pedals, the middle pedal is usually a sostenuto pedal.'Sostenuto' in Italian means 'sustained'. It is probably not the best term for the middle pedal, as it only sustains the notes that are being held down as the pedal is depressed, allowing future notes that are played to be unaffected.

On some upright pianos the middle pedal has a different function. If it is not a sostenuto pedal it will be a practise pedal. It can be slid to one side to lock it on. Doing this usually moves a curtain of felt down so that it is placed between the hammers and the strings. It means that you will be playing much more quietly, and this can be useful if it is necessary for you not to annoy family members or neighbours whilst you practise. Unfortunately the sound it makes it not nearly so satisfying when the practise pedal is in place, but you may nevertheless find it useful on some occasions.

Whether your piano has two or three pedals, the pedal on the left is known as the una corda pedal, or more commonly the soft pedal.

'Una corda' is another Italian term meaning 'one string'. On a grand piano the soft pedal shifts the entire action slightly to one side so that the hammers strike one less string per note, (some notes have three strings), and this creates a sound which is more muted.

If all this sounds complicated to you, that is because it is! A piano is a very complex instrument. It's a good idea to open up the top of your acoustic piano and take a look inside, so that you can see all the moving parts. Notice how the strings alter in width from the left to the right of the piano and watch what happens when you depress notes and pedals.

Modern digital pianos almost always have three pedals and the effect when you use them is exactly the same. However the middle pedal will always be a sostenuto pedal. A digital piano has no use for a practice pedal as you can alter the volume to very quiet using a simple control. How digital piano pedals actually work to achieve the same effects as the pedals of acoustic pianos, I have absolutely no idea! An acoustic piano pedal works by engaging or disengaging with the piano strings. As a digital piano has no strings but depends on electronic impulses, well your guess as to how the pedal works is as good as mine. Just be content that it does work, and works well.

It is worth considering getting a metronome when you start to play the piano. If you have got a digital piano a metronome will already be incorporated into the electronics and it is there to use at the press of a button. Failing that there are free apps you can get for your phone. If however you prefer something more stylish you will probably have seen and be familiar with the old fashioned triangular shaped metronome which you wind up and set the arm moving with the famous "tick tock". Some people think they are not as accurate as a digital one, but they certainly look smart sitting by your piano. As for accuracy, they are good enough for most amateur use. They don't come cheap, but are usually very reliable, having a wind up mechanism. A metronome helps the pianist keep time, and also gives an idea as to the speed composers had in mind when they wrote their music. As a beginner it will also help you to slow things down whilst you are still learning a piece, and then to gradually increase the speed as you become more proficient.

Some people like to have a light on their piano. You can get ones that are especially made for this purpose and they can be set at an angle that successfully lights your music. Depending on what other lighting you have in your room, this is something that you might find helpful.

A sharpened pencil and a good pencil rubber are always useful, so keep them near your piano so that you don't have to hunt for them when you need them. Also find an exercise book so that you can keep a record of your piano progress. Looking back through it from time to time will be an encouragement to you when you discover how far you have come.

Now, you are all ready to start your piano journey!

Where do you begin?

You've just got yourself an instrument to play on, or maybe a piano you already had has been newly tuned, and you can't wait to start. So where do you begin to learn how to make music?

The answer to this will be a very individual thing. Everyone will have different starting points depending on what experience, if any, they have had already.

If you feel you would make most progress with a teacher now is the time to look at some adverts, listen to any opinions others may give you, and book a trial lesson. You need to establish whether a particular teacher seems to understand where you are at, and what your aims are in learning the piano as a retired person. It's a good idea to think carefully, and write down, any thoughts and questions you might have, because, a bit like going to the doctor a lot of what you have previously thought you wanted to find out seems to vanish when you are there.

If you feel you want to proceed after your trial lesson, find out if you need to purchase any books. Some teachers have their own supply of tutor books which they lend out. This can be useful because in the early stages you may well progress fairly rapidly through the beginner books.

If you are intending to learn piano using the classical route, there are some suggestions of books which are especially geared to adults in the appendix at the end of this book.

A good teacher for you will be one who has experience of teaching adults. Not all teachers have that experience so do make sure you ask the right questions. The teacher should understand the sort of music you want to play and gear your lessons towards reaching your goals. So it is quite likely your route will be different from a child who is just beginning, working their way up through the graded system of exams. You may of course want to take exams yourself. Some adults do, especially if they are people who function best with the added pressure of a challenge ahead. But if you don't want to go down that route, say so at the beginning.

Your ideal teacher will of course be a good pianist him or her self, but will also be someone who can understand another person's difficulties. Patience is an essential quality for any piano teacher and also the ability to be able to balance constructive criticism with the right level of encouragement. Don't forget to ask what your teacher will charge for your lessons. There will be a national guideline which most people will follow when arranging their fee, but bear in mind there could be some variables. For instance, if you live near someone who is a renowned concert pianist, who also teaches, you can expect that person's fees to be much higher than a university music student. The student may actually be very good and could well charge less than the national average, so this may be a good option if the cost of lessons seem very high.

A teacher could also charge you more if they come to your house, rather than you going to theirs. This is because they would add on their travel cost, and also the extra time it would take them, time during which they could be teaching someone else. It is usually better for you to go to the home of your teacher, (or wherever else they teach – some rent a room just for their piano students). Also there are advantages to playing on a different piano from your own because it is good to get used to the feel of a different instrument from the beginning.

Hopefully you will find the ideal person to teach you, and when you do, stick to that person. A good piano teacher is like gold! Also, do your bit in keeping up a good relationship with your teacher. Be punctual for lessons. He or she may have other students before or after you.

If for any genuine reason you cannot attend a lesson on a certain day be sure to give at least 24 hours notice, and longer if possible. Of course, any decent person is going to make allowances for a real emergency, or sudden illness, but just not turning up for a lesson can be very frustrating for your teacher.

Many teachers now work on a system of payment in advance for a certain number of weeks. Maybe you will be asked to pay per quarter, ie 13 weeks. If you do not attend for a genuine reason most teachers will try to rearrange the lesson for you with no further payment. However, if you simply fail to turn up, do not expect a refund. If for any reason your teacher cannot be available for a lesson you will not be charged of course, but the missed lesson will be rearranged.

For teachers who take payment at the time of the lesson, it is especially important to give advance warning of weeks when you cannot attend. It is part of the teacher's livelihood, and pupils who skip lessons, and therefore payment, are one of the frustrations that private piano teachers have to cope with. If you simply forget to take your money one week, make absolutely sure you take double the next time you go.

Another thing that piano teachers find very frustrating is having pupils who do not practise from one week to the next. This happens more with children than with adults, and in retirement it is highly likely that you will practise as you are so keen to learn. However, for all of us life sometimes gets in the way, and despite your good intentions there are bound to be some times when you simply haven't had the time to play your piano. Be sure to tell your teacher at the beginning of the lesson if this has been the case. He or she will be able to tell anyway, but will appreciate honesty.

Do you really need a teacher? I am the first to say that if you can find a good teacher that you get on well with, this really is the best way to learn piano. Having said that, there has never been a better time than now to teach yourself, and if you look at YouTube you will see the results of some amazing people who have taught themselves, often with the help of modern technology. To quote the composer Paderewski, who was actually self taught himself, he once said that *'all piano students actually taught themselves -a teacher can only show them what to do'*.

So search the internet for online teachers who can show you what to do. In fact there are so many different courses offered online now that it is quite confusing deciding how to choose which one will suit you best. There are literally thousands of videos on YouTube showing you exactly what to do, geared to whatever stage you are at, starting with the complete beginner. Many of these are free, you can access them whenever you want, and of course you can play them over again and again until you have really grasped what you are trying to learn.

I have taken some time to research quite a few of these and offer you my thoughts about them. First, a disclaimer—

I have absolutely no financial gain from recommending any of the courses that I mention here, or any of the books that I recommend in Appendix 1. I am simply sharing my thoughts with you as I might to any friend who asked my opinion.

As far as I can see, at least 90% + of online courses are American, while there are a few with Australian origin.

This needn't be a problem of course, but just be aware that when advertising their goods it seems to be the American style to give a lot of hype, much of which doesn't quite ring true. Don't be taken in by it. You will often find headlines such as *'Learn to play the piano in just three weeks even if you are a complete beginner!* Of course, what they really mean is that three weeks might just be enough time to get you learning three very basic chords, and put them to a simple well known melody. Actually, probably most complete beginners will need more than three weeks to become fluent even on a simple song, but maybe a very bright person could just do it. That doesn't mean they have learnt how to play the piano. Far from it, for if you were to show them another piece of music most likely they won't have a clue.

Along with headlines like that you will also find, almost without exception, that they show you a high price for what they say their course is really worth, and then there will be dollars slashed out two or three times, until you come to the price they are offering it to you today. Only for today of course. If you don't act quickly you will miss it, and will have to pay much much more if you leave it for a week to think about it. Well, don't believe it! I have seen many courses offered like this, and the low price continues month after month, year after year. It just seems to be the way American sales people do business, and maybe it works well for them, even if a few of us in other parts of the world find it frustrating.

So look beyond the hype, don't worry about missing today's amazing deal (unlikely!), and try to find out what their teaching style is and what is really on offer. The vast majority of them will have videos which will show you their way of teaching, and if you look at some of these videos you may find some of them irritating, some talk too much, some go too fast, but others are excellent. They will hit a level that you feel is just right for you, and you will warm to their style.

Recently I have found many online teachers who will help you to learn a simple way of playing the piano. Some even offer Skype lessons, or group Zoom lessons, so if you have the technology to use it you might find this the best way to go. Below are a few, but you will find many more.

PianoVideoLessons is well worth looking at. No hype here, and Lisa who is the teacher has put a great deal of work into creating hundreds of videos, many of which are free to watch. There is a small charge if you want to print out the music in pdf form, and this is a good idea if you are serious about learning. In fact she has a scale of charges, from nothing at all, to a small charge for pdfs and an annual fee which gives you instruction which you can follow for many months. If you only want to follow the free lessons she gently asks if you will subscribe to supporting her via Patreon, and gives a scale of charges to suit every purse. However there is no pressure to do this, it's just a suggestion, and as she is a very good teacher I am sure many people do subscribe out of gratitude to her.

You can of course just work through all of her free lessons, many of which you can access on YouTube, though really it's as well to register with her and sign in, especially if you want to ask any questions. She always answers emails. More recently she has opened up interactive group lessons which you pay for and access on line at a time when others are there to share their progress with others and with Lisa.

There are other teachers who create very good videos, including plenty of free ones, such as another Lisa. This is Lisa Witt, of **Pianote**, who has also created lots of videos, some of which are instruction in many favourite songs, but others are explaining various aspects of technique, how to use the pedal, the best way to practise scales and so on. Then there is Thomas Werdemusiker of **PianoKomplete.** Thomas is German, but speaks and writes very good English. You pay and register for his course.

Also, Marina of **ThePianoKeys.com** does some wonderful free lessons, and has created lots of simple arrangements to popular songs. You do have to pay the small charge to be able to download the music, but it is well worth doing so, and sometimes you need to pay a little extra to get full tuition of just that one piece. However this will cost a lot less than signing up to a whole course which might contain music that you don't really like.

One great plus of learning piano in retirement is that you only ever need to learn to play music that you love. Compare this to those who have struggled with piano exams, having to study pieces that they really disliked. No wonder many people abandon piano as soon as they are able. But in later life, playing the piano should be fun. It should in fact be *playing*, not *drudgery.* If you always make sure you are enjoying what you play, you are unlikely to give it up.

Another big advantage of learning the piano using online instruction is that you can play the videos over and over again. When you go to an ordinary piano lesson it can often be difficult to remember all that was said, but re-running a video is so simple. Some videos might go too fast for you, but there are some that you are able to slow down to give you time to understand what is being taught on the piano. Although at one time it might have seemed extremely challenging to learn piano without going out to a teacher, the internet has radically changed that. Some online teachers are very good indeed, and equally important, you don't need to stick with just one. There are literally hundreds of piano tutorials on YouTube, free to watch, on almost every tune you may ever want to play.

One system that I want to mention which is rather different from those mentioned above is called **Pianoforall.** This is a very popular course written by an Irishman, Robin Hall. It has been around a few years now but seems to be as popular as ever. You can scroll through the huge amount of reviews he has received online, and they are impressive.

Pianoforall asks for a modest one time only fee of $37. For that you get eight eBooks, and embedded in the books, which once you have registered you can download, are videos which show you exactly how to play what you are being taught.

Let me tell you about my experience with Pianoforall. The books cover many aspects of piano playing, from absolute beginners, and leading on to using chords, and playing from a lead sheet. There are books on blues, jazz, and also on 'Taming the Classics', ballads, and playing by ear, to name just a few.

I subscribed to this course about seven years ago, and I think it was fairly new then. The books, which I could download and print were very good, but unfortunately none of the videos would work. I emailed Robin Hall, and he suggested I get 'quickplayer' on my computer. I did this, but still could not play the videos. However I learnt quite a bit from the books, and deciding it was my computer that was at fault, being quite old at that time, I didn't follow it up any further.

More recently I again looked at Pianoforall, and reading through the reviews I once more felt frustrated that I could never play the videos. I decided to contact Robin Hall again, and emailed him one Sunday evening about 8pm. Amazingly he emailed back within minutes! He told me that he had just renewed all the material, and asked me to register again, saying that if I then tried again to download them, they should work for me. I was impressed by his response as I fully expected to pay something extra as there had been a gap of seven years since I had first signed up for this course. But he told me simply to register again with nothing more to pay. I did this, and now the videos work for me! So I have to say I do recommend that you look at Pianoforall. It is not too expensive, but very comprehensive, and there is no doubt that Robin Hall is a real person who treats his customers well.

Piano Marvel is very popular, and certainly worth looking at. This gives you in their own words 'thousands of songs to learn to play, plus over 3,000 piano exercises at all levels'. You have to register with them and answer the question as to what level you are at. They will then suggest music which will be of the most help to you.

I also want to mention here a rather unique book by James Rhodes, called **'How to play the piano'**. James Rhodes is a concert pianist, born in London in 1975. He has a website www.jamesrhodes.tv.

The title of the book is maybe a little misleading, because he doesn't teach you to play the piano from the beginning, in the normal way, but rather how to play just one piece of music. It's not just any piece of music either, but a masterpiece by Johann Sebastian Bach, and he claims that you can do this in just six weeks, even if you have never touched a piano in your life before. What's more James

Rhodes claims you can achieve this by giving it just forty five minutes practising time each day, with a day off each week.

It's a bold claim to make. The music he has chosen is Bach's Prelude No. 1 in C major, and it's just thirty five bars long. It's a beautiful piece, and it can appear deceptively simple. Each bar has only 8 different notes in it and it is very repetitive. I don't know whether anyone has ever achieved the goal of learning this music in such a short time, but the book is worth studying because James's method of teaching is good and you can apply his system to any other music you may come across.

He shows you how to break it down into simple sections, learning just a few notes at a time, and not moving on until you can play those notes with the correct fingering, (which he gives you.) So to begin with you spend the whole of your first forty-five minutes on Bar 1. In this time you will be able to imprint this much on your mind, which is how he calculates the six week target for learning the whole piece, so if you are really determined, maybe it works. I should think that if you do manage to learn by this method you would then be wise to find a teacher who will take you through all the aspects of learning the piano which have not been touched on in this book. But maybe it's enough for some people that they can just play one beautiful piece of music. I suspect though that most people will not be content to leave it there.

I mentioned earlier on that my son taught me a simple way of playing the piano. He picked up this method from taking lessons on an electronic keyboard, which basically gives you a simple melody line to play with the right hand, and adding chords in the left hand. He was fortunate then to have a teacher who showed him how to adapt this method so that he could apply it to the piano, and I was astonished at how much he was able to play with very little formal piano training. I then discovered a book called **'How to play the piano in 10 easy lessons'** by Norman Monath, and I was pleased to find that this method was exactly what my son had been showing me.

Norman Monath worked for the publishers Simon & Schuster, and they published song books by well known songwriters such as Gershwin, Cole Porter, Rogers and Hammerstein to name a few. He explains that as his job was music editor he had a piano in his office, and sometimes he played it just for pleasure. Often colleagues would tell him they would 'give anything to be able to play some of those songs'. He insisted that it was not necessary to give *anything*. In fact in just a few lunch hours he could teach them everything they needed to know to play their favourite songs.

At first, he says, no-one believed him, but those that did take him up on his offer came to realise that to play simple melodies and chords of popular songs, hymns, Christmas carols or folk songs, required *'no talent and very little dexterity'*. So delighted were they with their new found skills they encouraged him to put all the information down in a mail order course, explaining his system, so that many more people could learn his method. For various reasons he was not able to do this, but many years later he put the information down in a book.

Norman Monath believed that playing the piano should be fun as well as a serious profession. He was aware though that most children are taught piano as if they were training to become concert pianists, and this method frightened many of them off. They abandoned it as soon as they were allowed to do so, and then as adults found they could not play anything, but regretted for much of their lives that they didn't stick at it as a child. So if you want to learn to play the piano just for sheer enjoyment, this book could be a very good starting point for you. I can recommend can it.

When you have tried out this system for a while I suggest that you then move on to another couple of books which expand the system further by showing in greater detail how to use chord inversions, and also different ways you can make the chord accompaniment more interesting. Both these books have the same title, **'How to play from a fake book'**. One is by Blake Neely and other by Michael Esterowitz. Both books pick up from the very basic skill of chord piano, so you do need to have a little experience before moving on to either of these instructions, but learning from these authors when you are ready will take your playing to a whole new level. If you decide to buy either of these books be sure to state that it is the keyboard edition that you need. Guitarists also use fake books, but their version of the book would be no use to you.

A fake book, by the way, is not a 'fake' at all. It is a real music book usually packed with hundreds of songs which give only the melody line and chord accompaniment, and is often called playing from a lead sheet. How you interpret this music is up to you. Play it the way that brings you most enjoyment. There are no rules.

Practise makes perfect
– or does it?

Whichever method you decide to pursue, whether this involves going out to a teacher, using online videos and lessons, or teaching yourself entirely on your own simply following the instructions in a tutor book, one thing is certain, you will need to practise.

Whatever anyone tells you, it is impossible to gain any real proficiency on piano without putting the work in, so adverts that tell you that you can learn piano in 21 days are simply misleading. In fact, it doesn't matter how many months, or even years, you learn the piano for, you will never stop learning.

Do you really need to learn scales? You may remember how you hated them if you are a retiree who learnt the piano as a child, and you don't want to visit them again. The truth is that you may be able to make some progress without them, but there is no doubt that learning to play scales accurately will be of enormous help to you. In fact, why not learn to love them? You will find books and videos today which show you interesting ways to play them, so look out for some of these. There is no need to spend hours learning scales, unless you are thinking of taking piano exams, but it is a good idea to always start your practise sessions playing a few scales. Think of it as a warm up, just as sports people warm up before a game. Also, if ever you are asked to play on a piano that you are not used to, a few scales are the ideal way to get the feel of it. Pianos are very individual instruments, and they all feel slightly different, and some people find this off-putting until they get used to it.

When you are learning scales play each hand separately first, and make sure that you can play each hand perfectly before putting them together. The first time you play both hands together can be quite challenging. Your brain will have stored the fingering for each hand separately, and now you are asking it to mix the two different parts without making any mistakes. It's not as easy as you might think.

This doesn't just apply to scales. The key to learning any new piece of music involves four things of great importance.

1) Before you begin, always look at the key signature. This will tell you how many sharps or flats, if any, are needed, and also how many beats in a bar. Forgetting to look for this information before you begin will ruin your first attempts at playing a new piece.

2) Always play each hand separately at first, for the reasons suggested above.

3) Observe any suggested fingering. These have been added by an experienced pianist as being the best way to

play this particular piece, and you will usually find these fingering suggestions will help you with any otherwise difficult moves around the piano. Remember though that these are only suggestions, and as peoples' hands are different shapes and sizes, slightly different fingering in some passages might work better for you. If this is so feel free to change it. Be sure to mark your copy with the fingering that you find easiest, but once you have got that sorted, stick to it! This is very important as it will help your brain to remember the best way to achieve accuracy.

4) Learn just a couple of bars at a time, or even just one bar, and play it very very slowly. When you think you are already playing it slowly, go even slower, so slowly that every note you play is exactly what is written, no mistakes at all. When you can play those bars, however few, at a slow speed without any mistakes, speed it up a little. If you make a mistake, go back to playing very slowly.

Once you can play a little bit faster with no mistakes, go on to the next couple of bars, and concentrate on these in the same fashion. Then put the first bars you learnt together with these, and when you are successful, add another couple. For variety you might like to try these same passages with the left hand, on it's own at first, very slowly, but when you are able, play both hands together. This often feels difficult at first, and you might have to go back to the ultra slow pace when you begin to play both hands together, but that's fine. As the saying goes, 'slow and steady wins the race'.

This method might sound very tedious to you, but it will save you time in the long run, for this is the way to becoming note perfect, and playing a piece beautifully and with confidence. This chapter title questioned whether practise really does make perfect, as we are led to believe. In fact, what practise actually does is make something permanent. If you keep on playing wrong notes, that is what will be imprinted on your brain, and you want to avoid this at all costs. It's the correct notes with the best fingering that your brain needs to store.

Once you have learnt the notes of a piece, both hands together, you can then begin to think about the dynamics, putting your own expression and feelings into a piece, and making it your own. It's very difficult to do this if you are still at the stage of learning notes and making mistakes.

However, I am not suggesting that you need always to be absolutely note perfect. There is a skill in carrying on playing even when you make a mistake. Even professional pianists make some mistakes but you probably never notice it. When you are at the stage of beginning to learn a piece you need to pay attention to detail and be as accurate as possible. Once you are able to put both hands together, playing it musically is more important than absolute correctness, so don't let the odd mistake worry you. Just be sure to keep going.

It can be difficult when you are learning the piano to assess yourself correctly as to how you are progressing. Most people are far too critical of themselves, and however good they are they always feel they could have been/should have been better. In fact this is one of the big differences between a young child learning the piano, and a retiree learning. Few adults are ever truly satisfied with their own piano playing, but at our time of life this seems a shame.

One way to ensure you are making progress is to buy some grade exam music. If you are not wanting to take any exams this doesn't have to be the music for the current exams. If you look on Amazon or eBay you will find graded music from years back that you can purchase very cheaply indeed. Try working your way through some of this music, starting with grade one, and progressing to the higher grades as time passes. If you are playing the piano most of all for a fulfilling hobby you should be able to feel satisfaction and joy in realising how far you have come since you started.

So first of all, learn to play a very simple piece beautifully, and don't despise it for it's simplicity.

Incidentally, for those who play the traditional method and would like to improve their sight reading, these grade exam books which can be bought very cheaply are an excellent resource. Just get the books that are some grades lower than your actual standard. You don't need the CD's for this purpose, although if you are trying to teach yourself it might be a good idea to get them so that you can check whether you have played the music correctly. Don't be tempted to listen to it first though. True sight reading means just that – playing something that you have never seen or heard before, and getting the notes and the timing right first time. It's a great skill to have.

Some time ago now I was very impressed by the internationally famous flute player James Galway. I heard him play the simple Londonderry Air, and it was very noticeable that he put as much care and passion into playing that tune as he would have if he had been playing a complicated Mozart sonata. It occurred to me then that this attitude had contributed to his greatness, and it seemed a good lesson for all musicians to learn.

It is possible that you will sometimes find when you have been practising a particular piece for a long time, you get somewhat bored with it and feel that you are not making any progress. When this happens, and it is quite likely that it will from time to time, leave that music for a while and move on to something else, some new challenge, maybe something a little more difficult. Come back to the previous piece when a few weeks have passed, and you might be pleasantly surprised at how well you are doing. I don't know why this works, but I have certainly found it to be true.

When they first start to learn to play the piano people sometimes ask how long they should practise for, and do they have to practise every day. Experts usually agree that a short time, even 15 minutes a day is far better than a couple of hours just once a week.

In any case if you are just beginning it's probably not a good idea to spend too long at the piano. While you may think you are only using your fingers to play the notes, in fact your whole body becomes involved. It is important not to overdo your practise time as you certainly don't want to end up with any sort of repetitive strain injury. So pace yourself. Probably 20 to 30 minutes a day would be a good length of time to begin with. Or you could do 20 minutes in the morning and then again later on in the day.

In fact this would make a very good pattern. When you are really enjoying your piano it is so easy to let time run away with you. Even on days when you don't really feel much like it you will find that, once you begin it becomes very difficult to stop. Time simply flies! So it's a good idea to set a timer at the start of your practise session. Do this even if you have nothing else in particular to do, because you will find a few minutes break away from practise most refreshing.

Always start each practise session with a 'warm up'. This could be some scales, or even a simple tune you have been learning that you can play easily and well. After that it is also a good idea to divide your practise time up into sections, and here again your timer might be useful. Give the first five minutes to warming up with something simple. If your particular warm up has been a scale, add another one, this time one you are finding more difficult, or add some chords or arpeggios (meaning the notes of the chord played separately).

Next you need to work on something that you are at the stage of only just learning. This should be something that is perhaps a little more difficult than other music you are playing, something that challenges your brain to work a bit harder. Break the piece up into sections, learning just two or three bars at a time. The next day, providing you have remembered what you learnt the day before, add another three bars, and carry on until you have learnt the whole piece. You could perhaps allow fifteen minutes on this new music.

Give the last ten minutes to playing the music that you love, that you play best, that makes you happy. Always try to finish each practise session with something that sounds good to you and that you enjoy, so that you end up feeling positive. Before you know it the timer will ring, and all too soon you will be at the end of your practise session, already looking forward to the next time you can sit at your beloved piano.

What if you feel you haven't time to practise for 20-30 minutes a day? For some people with busy lives that might seem like a long time to begin with. Before you feel that it's impossible it's worth thinking about how you spend your days. Do a time and motion study, and for a couple of days keep a record of how much time you spend doing all the usual things you have to do. When you have done this, can you find a slot for just 10 minutes a day? If you allow yourself 10 minutes a day for six days of the week, and have one day without any practise at all, you have still managed a whole hour of practise, and as previously said, many experts tell us that this is better than playing for an hour on only one day of the week. If you feel this would work for you, be sure to set a timer, because I can promise you that before you know it, once you sit down at your piano, however much you may not feel like it, when you get started twenty minutes will be gone before you know it. This is much more likely to happen for adults than for young children, some of whom can't wait to get the dreaded practise out of the way so they can go out to play. This is also the reason why older people just starting the piano often make faster progress than children, so you can be glad that at least for this part of your life, time really does just fly!

It's worth keeping a record of how you spend your practise time, and this is where the exercise book mentioned earlier comes in handy. Think of what goals you are trying to reach in a given time. Make sure your goals are achievable. If they are too ambitious you may become disheartened, but reaching even a small goal gives a boost to your well being. Teachers will often give children a star for small achievements. You could get some stars and stick them in your own book. After all, why not? Everyone needs an ego boost sometimes.

It needs to be said here that whatever route you take to learning to play the piano, whether it's the traditional method or the easier chord way, practising is still very important. That is why some of the adverts which suggest that you can learn to play the piano in an unbelievably short time are very misleading. There are after all many parts of learning to play that require your brain to store new information, to create new nerve pathways from brain to hand, to build muscle strength in fingers that are being asked to do something new in perfecting finger dexterity, to name but a few. It won't happen overnight, but slowly and steadily, week by week, month by month, you will notice that you have begun to move forward.

It's very useful to look back at your progress over a longer period of time, and hopefully you can be really pleased with yourself when you discover just how much progress you have made, and how many stars you were able to give yourself.

Make the Music Your Own

One big difference between a child learning to play the piano at the age of 6 or 7, and someone of retirement age just beginning, is that you as an adult know the sort of music you love. You have a whole wealth of tunes stored in your subconscious. Some of them are favourites that you listen to often and never tire of. Others may have appealed to you once, but not any longer. One thing is certain, you have moved far beyond some of the set pieces in piano tutor books. To a child it is all new. They have no idea what the pieces are meant to sound like, and so a teacher will take them through many different styles to give them a good all round music education.

Maybe you have been thinking 'If only I could play just that one song on the piano', or 'I wish I could just sit down at the piano and play my favourite tunes'.

It's partly because many piano tutor books are unsatisfactory for adults, that some people get disheartened early on, and feel they are never going to be able to play the music they love.

This is why I am very much in favour of YouTube tutorials. You can find instruction at your level on hundreds of tunes, ranging from popular songs, and even some classical music.

Purists will not be in favour of easy versions of some of the works of the great Masters, but why not? It seems a shame not to be able to play a piece just because you are not allowed an easy version. Even though admittedly rearranging some difficult pieces to be played in an easier key than that in which it was written alters the intrinsic feel of the music, nevertheless the essential melody that you love is still there. Promise yourself that the more experienced you become you can look forward to the day when you will be proficient enough to attempt some of these great works in their original form, but for now, just enjoy playing them at your own level.

Here I must say something about that word 'easy'. It is a relative term, and what is easy to a beginner, and easy to an intermediate player or beyond, are two very different things. Also, the standard of easy music varies considerably. Some sound thin and frankly not very good, whilst others are excellent. This is another advantage of YouTube as you can hear the version you might be about to attempt played before you commit yourself. If the end result sounds good, then go for it!

So the first rule of making the music your own is play only what you love. The second rule is, never be afraid to mark your music, adding reminders of the fingering, accidentals (sharps and flats), when to add expression etc. This is where your pencil and rubber come in handy. I know that some people prefer to rub out their reminders when they feel they have committed them to memory. I more often find myself adding even more reminders, and highlighting some parts when I find some things difficult to remember. It's surely one of the perks of learning piano as an older adult!

For people who like to keep their music in pristine condition, I have another suggestion. Amazon and eBay have a huge amount of music in their used markets. Just recently I bought two second hand copies of a book I owned that I loved. You will find that in most books, only a few pieces will be played often, and many will hardly ever be looked at. I cut out of these two used copies the pieces I wanted to keep, and I put these copies into plastic polypockets in a project binder. It took two used copies, because that meant I could place the appropriate sheets back to back, thus eliminating the need to have parts of music in my own book that I would probably never play. I mark these copies in whatever way I find most helpful, and of course I still have my original 'good' copy which remains unspoilt.

I can recommend another tip to you, whether you are using just sheet music, books of music, or polypockets as suggested above. Page turning when you are alone can be difficult, but make a tag at the bottom of the page that needs to be turned. To do this you need a roll or sheet of peel off sticky labels. Cut a small strip, about 1 cm width, and stick it onto the bottom of the page, folding it back so that it sticks on both sides of the plastic pocket containing the page you want to turn, but leaving about three centimetres beyond the bottom right of the page. The folded label will then stick to itself, giving you a convenient lever for quickly turning a page. You can do this whether you are keeping the pages of your music in polypockets, in which case attach the sticker onto the outer plastic, or if your music is loose or in a book, attach the stickers to the paper pages. Either way, it really does make page turning much easier.

In this way you could make up your own books on different types of music. For example, keep popular songs in one binder, Christmas carols in another, classical pieces in their own book, and so on. It is good to have your music organised, otherwise you waste time hunting for whatever you want to play.

Keeping all your favourite music together adds to your enjoyment of playing the piano. The more you love the pieces the more you will enjoy playing them. The more you enjoy playing them the more accomplished you will become. The more your playing improves, the more satisfaction it will give you. The more satisfaction in playing you have, the more you will love your piano playing.

But please, always remember that photocopying music is illegal, unless you have been give specific permission to photocopy anything downloaded from the internet. Some of these will already be free. Those that you have paid for will usually have your name printed at the foot of each page, showing that it is legal.

Performance

When people know that you are learning to play the piano, sooner or later someone is bound to ask you to play something for them. If you are used to playing on your own, maybe even when there is no-one in the house but yourself, this can be quite daunting. Playing the piano for others is very different from playing on your own.

I have called this section 'performance', but I am not suggesting you will be 'performing' anything at a very early stage in your piano journey. The problem is though that even playing something simple for other people to listen to can be very nerve racking, and you might even experience something akin to stage fright.

The quotation *"Do the thing you fear and the death of fear is certain" (Ralph Waldo Emerson)* has some truth in it here. The more you play for other people the easier it gets, and the more confident you become. But some people find playing for others makes them so anxious they avoid it altogether.

It seems easier for young children to play for others than for adult beginners to do so. This is because adults are much more critical of themselves than children are. Adults have a far clearer idea in their minds of what they should sound like, and so they get much more bothered about people hearing their imperfections. In fact the fear of playing for others is largely the fear of other people hearing your mistakes. How wonderful it would be if you could always sound perfect!

Remember that mistakes are a normal part of learning to play the piano, but it's also a fact that the more anxious you are about them the more mistakes you make. People who go regularly to a piano teacher will tell of the frustration of being able to play well a piece that they have practised at home, only to find that when they get to their teacher and they are now on a different piano they make several mistakes, so it doesn't sound anything like as good as it did at home.

Do not worry! Piano teachers are well aware of this problem, and they can tell for sure whether you have practised or not since your last lesson. It's natural to be far more relaxed when you play the piano at home alone. Playing for your teacher, and perhaps even more for friends sometimes causes you to become tense, and this increases the chances of playing wrong notes, or even losing your place in the music. Because you know of another person's presence, or others in the room with you, part of your brain becomes aware of them instead of concentrating on what you are doing. You feel very self conscious, and you can't focus on the music you are playing.

How do you overcome this problem? There is no easy answer, but there are some tips to help your manage your nerves and keep them under control. To begin with, don't try to play something for other people that is too challenging for you. Keep a simple piece that you play well always ready. By that I mean something that you learnt to play well early on in your piano journey, that is easy for you now, but a piece that you like. Visit this piece often, maybe keep it as the warm up that you play at the beginning of every practice session. The more you know it, the easier it will be to play for others. In fact, you should know this music so well it becomes almost automatic, and this will give you confidence.

If possible, try to record yourself playing this piece. This is easy if you have a digital piano, but most people have some technology these days which allows them to record, maybe even on your phone. The first time you do this you may be surprised how different it feels when you are recording yourself from when you are just at your normal practice session. When you play it back you might well surprise yourself at how good it sounds.

Don't be over concerned about the odd mistake. When you are learning a piece it is important not to keep on practising mistakes, but when you are thinking of playing for others it is time to learn the art of carrying on through any mistakes. Most people won't even notice them anyway, and but even if they do they will soon forget about them.

One tip that might be worth trying – have a talk show on the radio or television on at a fairly loud volume whilst you are playing. This will help you to concentrate on your music even with the background distraction, and it is so much easier than playing for others when you can almost hear a pin drop. As you can become quite self conscious when you first start playing for others this can make you lose your concentration and therefore make mistakes. So see if this tip works for you. Playing with distracting background sounds will improve your ability to concentrate on the music you are playing.

However you go about it, the more you play for others the more confident you will become. So believe in yourself. You can do it.

The final part of this chapter is for those who attend a place of worship, and may want to play the piano there. If this doesn't apply to you feel free to move on to the next chapter.

I wanted to add a section on playing in church, because pianists are often hard to come by. The churches often give people, young and old, an experience of playing for others which you will not find in other organisations. Sometimes the regular pianist or organist cannot be there for a certain Sunday, or suddenly he/she announces that they are moving to another town and will no longer be available to play. Some churches have then to resort to singing unaccompanied, or perhaps more often now, singing to recorded music. Well, that is better than nothing, but it in no way compares to having a pianist. It doesn't matter if you have never played an organ. Playing the piano will do just as well, and most churches have at least access to a portable digital piano which you can use.

You may be tempted to find some music books which are a collection of 'easy' to play hymns, or Christmas Carols, but beware! Whilst some hymns in these books may be suitable, others will be set in an easy to play key which then makes them either much too high or too low for people to sing to. It is far better to learn to play from a proper hymn book from the start.

A glance at any old fashioned hymn book might seem rather scary at first, and there is no doubt that playing hymns in four part harmony as printed requires a skill level which you may not yet have achieved. But there is an easier way. Find a hymn book which provides the guitar chords for every hymn. The popular book *Mission Praise* does this for every hymn in the book, and you will find others have this facility if you look around for them.

Play the melody line with the right hand, using only the top note and ignoring the chords that are written in the treble clef. With the left hand, play the guitar chords, which are written above the notes which you will be playing. Usually you will change chords as they are written, but in some instances far too many chords are given. Guitarists also find this. If you feel you have to play every single chord that is given it might seem too daunting for you, so just play the easy ones, leaving some out altogether if there seem to be too many. Cross out with a pencil the unnecessary chords so that they don't confuse you. You will quickly get the sense of which are the superfluous chords once you start to play the hymn.

Some of the chords will be easy to find but occasionally you may come across one you have not seen before. For speed it's a good idea to get a book of chords so that you can easily look up how to play the chord that is new to you. See the Appendix 1 for a suggestion of a useful book. You will often find though that it is the more complex chords that you really do not need, at least to begin with.

When you begin to play hymns this way use only the position where the root note is at the bottom of the chord. By that I mean that if, for instance, you are looking for the chord C, the root note of that chord is C, and that will be the lowest note you will play, In fact, if you are really just beginning, it will work if you play just the root note alone.

 Once you find out how easy this method is and you have had some time to develop it, you will be able to achieve a fuller sound by playing the full chord as written. The next step will then be learning chord inversions. Commit some of the most common chord inversions to memory, and it will take your hymn playing sound much more professional. For one thing you will be able to find common notes in chords, which means you will be often be able to change onto the next chord by moving only one or two fingers, rather than your whole hand, and this means that the whole effect will be smoother. Initially you only need to learn the chords shown in whatever hymn you are playing, but in time you will find you have a large number of chords stored away in your memory, so it becomes easy to play on sight.

You may also find that whilst some hymns work well with block chords (meaning all three or four notes of the chord played together), others sound better with arpeggios (the notes of the chord being played separately). So once you start to learn this method find a book, or again a YouTube teacher, who will show you how you can add interest by playing those chords in different ways. You will find some suggestions for various resources in the Appendix 1 at the end of this book.

This is in fact the same method talked about in a previous chapter on playing from a fake book. I know that many people will be extremely pleased when they discover how easy it is. There are bound to be others, of course, for whom nothing but the real thing will do. To those reading this who feel that the method discussed here is a poor substitute for playing in four part harmony, ignore this section and do what you feel is right for you. If you put enough time and work into it, anything is possible, and if you have previously, perhaps in your youth, been taught piano via the usual classical route, you already have the beginnings of learning to play some hymns as they are written. So you may feel that this 'correct' way will ultimately give you the most satisfaction. Everyone must decide to do what they feel is best and right for themselves.

However you decide to learn and play hymns you definitely need to find out how to use the sustain pedal. Once again, if you do not have a teacher search on YouTube for instruction on using the pedal. Correct use of the pedal will help you to achieve a much more professional sound, but don't fall into the trap of over using it. As noted in a previous chapter, if you fail to lift your foot off the pedal at the right time you will end up with a jumble of sound which won't sound nice at all.

The most important aspect of starting to play hymns in church is to keep going. Once singers have got off to a good start they should be able to keep going even if you only add a few chords here and there to keep them in tune. Whatever you do, don't stop when you make a mistake and then start at the beginning again. I say 'when' you make a mistake because most likely you will, but if you keep going most people won't even notice any errors.

There are many people who have started off playing the piano in church quite reluctantly, and very nervously, but it is marvellous how much their confidence grows, and how much they improve in a relatively short time. If you decide to try the chord method you will find it an amazingly easy way to play hymns and carols, and it is perfectly adequate for a congregation to sing to.

No one who is organising or leading a church service or meeting should expect you to play for the singing without giving you advanced warning of what they want you to play. So if you do get involved in playing at your place of worship you must insist on having the hymn numbers a few days in advance to give you time to practise them. In your early days of playing you could also suggest that you are given a couple of alternatives in case one of the chosen ones proves to be too difficult for you.

Playing in church is a wonderful way of sharing your hobby and skills with others. You will find it very satisfying and fulfilling, and the simple method of playing melody line and chords also works very well for Christmas carols and popular songs.

You could try it also for nursery rhymes. Perhaps there is a nursery school near where you live who would enjoy having a pianist to play these simple songs for them. Or there could be a Rainbow or Brownie Pack that would welcome you. Lots of children these days have no idea where music comes from, as they only ever hear recorded music played. We often hear of children who don't know where their basic food comes from, and sadly the same thing is happening with music. It will enrich their lives, seeing someone who is actually playing a piano for them, so don't be afraid to seek out every opportunity.

Also, if there is a residential care home near you that has a piano the residents will love to sing along to some of the songs they enjoyed years ago. There are many timeless songs that you can find in easy versions with appropriate chords shown making it possible for you to learn how to play them. It is a wonderful thing to share your piano skills with others and brighten their day.

Be aware that, quite rightly, safeguarding is taken very seriously today, and any volunteering with children or the elderly may require you to be DBS checked. But it will be worth it!

Health Problems

If you have reached retirement age and you have no health issues at all you are indeed very fortunate, so count your blessings daily! Most people have at least the odd one or two niggling conditions, so it seems right to address some of these, and the effect they may have on your piano playing.

It is quite likely that the majority of people over the age of about 45 will need some spectacles for reading, even if they have never needed to wear them before that age. If it is just reading glasses that you need you may find that reading the music in front of you is not easy. This is because your prescription will have been fixed for reading print at the distance at which you would normally read a newspaper or a book, and that could be nearer to you than the music on your piano. If you find this to be a problem speak to your optician. Some people have a special pair of spectacles just for reading music, which makes life much easier for them. If you wear contact lenses with spectacles for reading, again you may need different reading lenses for music from those you use for reading a book.

By the time you reach your sixties and beyond is quite likely that you will be wearing varifocals, or some people will prefer bifocals, but you may find that even these are not ideal for reading music, so again, do discuss the problem with an optician. It might be a good idea to take some music with you when you go for an eye test, and then the optician can see the correct distance that you need to be able to read music from, and prescribe accordingly. If one optician doesn't understand your problem, find another one who does!

Age related hearing loss deserves a mention in this chapter because of the way it might affect your piano playing. It is estimated that 40% of people over the age of 50 have some degree of hearing loss, and that figure rises to 70% to those aged 70 and above. Hearing loss is something that creeps up on older people very gradually, and usually they are not aware of it in the early stages. Also, many people try to hide it when they first become aware of it. They are likely to say that they can hear perfectly well but other people don't speak clearly these days.

The reason for this is that hearing loss is not simply about volume, but is more about the frequency levels of the spoken words. If you have age related hearing loss you will probably have loss in the high frequencies, and this is where the consonants are heard. If you are not hearing consonants clearly you will struggle to understand what is being said.

I never understand why people are much more self conscious about wearing hearing aids than they are of wearing spectacles. Hearing aids today are often so very discreet that most of the time no-body will notice you are wearing them. What they *will* notice however, probably even before you are aware of it yourself, is that you are mishearing things that are said to you, often asking people to repeat things, and needing the television turned up too loud. These are the things that make individuals appear to be showing signs of ageing, not the wearing of almost invisible hearing aids. In fact almost certainly there will be some people known to you who will be wearing hearing aids, but you have never noticed.

If you are aware that your hearing is not as acute as it once was, do not worry that you might be tone deaf. It would be very unusual for it to affect your ability to gauge the tones you are hearing, so don't be afraid to sing or be part of a choir. You can still do that. However you do need to be aware that hearing aids might affect how you hear your piano. In fact, it is unfortunate that acoustic pianos are not always ideal for wearers of today's digital hearing aids.

Digital hearing aids are so sensitive that sometimes they pick up the vibration of the strings as the piano hammers hit them when notes are depressed. This can make the wearer of the aids hear a 'twangy' sound, causing the piano to sound as though it needs tuning. It is very unfortunate for those who have a much loved piano to find this is happening. Some people try to wear the more old fashioned acoustic aids for piano playing, but these are extremely difficult to come by now. They probably would have to be made as a one off for you and would therefore be very expensive, even if you could find some firm that would actually make them for you.

There is no real answer to this, apart from admitting that, for hearing aid wearers, a digital piano might actually be a better option. You will find that some experienced piano dealers know this to be the case, and will actually recommend that you try a digital piano to see if this suits you better. If it gives you a more satisfactory sound then please don't despise this option, because if the sounds you are hearing from your acoustic piano are uncomfortable for you, you will not have much pleasure in playing it. Remember, playing the piano in retirement should always be fun and bring you joy, not displeasure or frustration.

Don't forget you are in good company if you have hearing loss. Beethoven struggled with progressive hearing loss, but wrote some of his finest music when any residual hearing had almost gone. Mind you, he did ruin some good pianos by playing them so forcefully to enable to hear himself, they sometimes gave way under the strain. That is one example you will not want to follow.

It is not uncommon for pianists to develop pain in their hands and wrists, and this is often the result of poor technique. A good piano teacher will notice tension in your hands and will help you to relax them. This will not only go a long way to preventing injury but will also enhance your playing.

If you do not have a teacher but are teaching yourself or using online lessons, Marina from **ThePianoKeys** has produced a video on Finger Independence, and says that if you invest some time every day in doing the exercises which she gives you which are targeted to get you playing in a healthy way, using the natural motions of your body, you will be able to play those beautiful pieces more easily. Whilst the video on YouTube is free to watch, online coaching sessions with Marina can also be arranged. With modern technology she is able to see the areas that need tweaking, so it is well worth booking a session with her to benefit from her expertise, and achieve pain free playing.

Arthritis is a different problem and is something that many people suffer from to some degree in later life. In fact, playing the piano could be very good treatment for you. There has always to be a balance between resting painful joints and also exercising them, but although piano playing will not cure the condition it could make the joints less painful, and slow down further deterioration. So don't think it's no use trying to play the piano. If in doubt, speak to a physiotherapist for expert advice on how much playing you should do at each session.

If you wonder how you will ever get your fingers to work, be inspired by some of the amazing people on YouTube who have overcome seemingly impossible disabilities to become wonderful pianists. Look for Darrius Simmons, who was born with only four fingers, or Nicholas McCarthy, who has become known as the one-handed pianist. There is also a Russian teenager who was born with no hands, but there is a stunning performance on YouTube of him playing the beautiful 'River flows in you' by composer Yiruma. How he manages to do this is almost beyond belief! It seems that nothing is impossible if you set your mind to it.

Other historical examples of people who have overcome severe arthritis and continued to play the piano are Clara Schumann, the widow of Robert Schumann. She was very badly affected by the painful condition, but in spite of that she continued to give piano concerts for the pleasure of huge audiences in Europe for many years. The composer Rachmaninoff also had severe pain in his finger joints, but continued to play wonderfully well, proving that with determination it is possible to play the piano, even with arthritis.

Back and/or neck pain is quite common in pianists of all ages, and often comes from bad posture at the piano. Make sure that your piano stool is at the right height for you to be comfortable. Of course, piano stools provide no back support. This may be fine if you only have a short time to play, but if you want to spend longer at your piano, I think, having reached retirement age, there is no reason why you shouldn't use a straight backed chair. If it has arm rests, so much the better, and so long as it is the right height for you, you may find this helpful. You will not be the first to do this, and in fact the pianist and composer Paderewski has been photographed sitting at his piano in an armchair. Experiment to find out what works best for you. If you really want to play the piano, you will find a way to make it a comfortable experience.

If you find that sitting regularly at the piano causes you pain or discomfort in your back or neck, don't ignore it, because it is a sign that something is wrong and needs fixing. If you have a piano teacher discuss the problem with him/her. A good teacher will be able to tell whether there are any faults in your posture which is causing you problems. If you do not have a teacher search for the solution on YouTube.

Do not spend too long sitting at the piano at each session, but rather get up after 20 minutes and take a walk away from the piano. It is a good idea to set a timer so that you can do this before any discomfort begins. After a short break you can then sit at the piano again for another 20 minutes, or whatever timing you find is comfortable for you.

For those who find that sitting at the piano regularly causes them back or neck pain, it might be a good idea to consult an Alexander Technique practitioner. There are some who specialise in posture for musicians, and lots of people have achieved very good results after just a few sessions with an expert who can show you how to align your spine when sitting at the piano.

When it comes to issues of the mind and mental health, . there have been many studies on the positive effects playing the piano has on children. In fact some have been so positive that there are schools in Sweden which insist that every child learns a musical instrument right up to the age of 16. They put us to shame, when in the UK and also the USA music education has been cut to the bare minimum, and learning an instrument has become largely only for those who have enough money to fund lessons for their children. This is a very sad situation, because education should never be only about passing GCSEs or whatever exams are the current favourites. Education should equip people for all aspects of life.

There is a saying attributed to Plato: *"I would teach children music, physics and philosophy; but most importantly music, for the patterns in music and all the arts are the keys to learning".*

An assistant professor of music education at the University of South Florida, Tampa, has studied the impact of learning the piano in later life, especially of people between the ages of 60 and 85. She has concluded that there are without doubt benefits for the brain even if you never learnt to play an instrument as a child but only begin to learn in later life. Her studies found that after 6 months, those who took piano lessons appeared to have better memories, were able to process information quicker, and had better planning ability and other cognitive functions, compared with those who had not received lessons.

This is very encouraging, because many people worry about memory loss in advancing years. They also feel that they are not able to learn anything new as they get older, but this is not true. The brain is always capable of learning new things. It has long been thought that learning a new language in retirement helps to keep the brain in good condition. Music is of course a language, and in particular playing the piano is quite a complex exercise.

You can believe therefore that playing the piano in retirement is not only a great hobby, but also a fantastic way to keep your brain exercised and sharp. It is also very good therapy for your mental health, for whilst you are grappling with some new music, the concentration required means that you are entirely focused in the present moment. This is true mindfulness, which we hear greatly benefits to our mental health, and it can help with dealing with depression. As has been said before, time flies when you are sitting at your piano. The more you play, the better you become, and the more you will be able to soothe away the stresses of the day with your music. Playing the piano is truly holistic.

For those suffering from depression or loneliness, learning to play the piano can be of huge value to their mental health. Concentrating on the music focuses your mind away from your problems and dark thoughts, and brings you into the present moment. When you are able to play some simple pieces well it can have a calming influence on your mind. Your self esteem is lifted, and if you do decide to play for others you will make good social contacts as well. There is nothing else quite like it.

In conclusion

I started this book by saying I was searching for the truth about whether it is possible to learn piano in retirement.

I have discovered that the answer to that is more complex than it seems at first. I am unable to give a simple yes or no answer. The truth is that it is dependent on so many things, such as what you want to achieve, what sort of music you most want to play, even what sort of person you are.

Let me clarify what has been discussed. If you love classical music and want to play any of the great works of the masters in the form in which they were written, you will have a long road ahead of you. I do believe that anything is possible, and very recently I heard of a man who started to learn to play the piano when he was 60 having never touched it before. At the age of 83 he was just about to take his Grade 8 exam. I know for a fact that this is a genuine story, and what an achievement! Also, what dedication he must have had. Other factors in his success include his personal mind set, focusing on his goals, more than likely having a very good piano, having lots of time for daily practise with very few distractions. In addition there is no doubt that he has had a very good teacher, or teachers, with whom he has forged an excellent working relationship. So it can be done.

I have also known other adults who started in retirement and reached Grade 4 before finally becoming disheartened, and feeling that it was beyond them to continue. Unfortunately this is also the story that lots of youngsters can relate to, and maybe even some readers of this book had the same experience in their youth.

It seems that the grade system works for some people but not others. If you are a very driven person, determined and always needing something to strive for there is no reason at all why you shouldn't take these exams in retirement, but be aware that it can and does put some people off completely. Part of the reason for this is that you will be having to play a lot of music which you don't like, alongside a few pieces that you do like of course. For some children music is simply another course of study and exam taking, alongside maths and geography etc. In other words, it is viewed as work rather than play.

If you have decided that you want to learn the piano using the traditional method, do try to find a teacher that you can work well with. I believe that this is essential if you hope to do grade exams, or even have a desire just to work towards playing some of the timeless, complex works of the great composers. This is because such music involves more than just hitting the right notes at the right time. You need to learn all aspects of technique, and you will start to realise that it is not just your fingers that are playing, but your whole body is subtly involved. The way you sit at the piano matters, the way you relax your wrists, move your arms, shape your fingers, all play a part in developing your musicality. Therefore it is necessary for a teacher to be actually with you to check on all these things.

Learning the piano via the traditional route is undoubtedly the best way of learning. So if what you really want is to play traditional music, or indeed any sort of music, and develop into an all round musician, that is the way to go. It will take a lot of time and dedication. There will be days when it is frustrating, when you feel like you are not getting anywhere, but whatever you do, don't give up too soon. Decide you are going to stick with it for as long as it takes.

Never forget though that in retirement the most important thing is that whatever course you take you 'play' the piano, and it should bring you great enjoyment, as well as a sense of achievement. If you just want to be able to make some music, don't despise the simpler route to playing the piano that has been mentioned in this book. If you long to play some favourite songs you can fairly quickly learn to do this using the chord approach. Then if in the future you decide to add the classical method to your skills, what you have learnt using this method will stand you in good stead.

Piano playing can sometimes feel to be quite a solitary occupation, so it's a good idea to join some groups of others to share experiences. If you are a Facebook user you will find there are groups on there which are free to join, some particularly geared to adult piano learners. Members come from a wide variety of experience, from total beginners to some who almost seem like professionals with a wealth of experience. They are often open to answering any questions you may have, so feel free to share your own experiences. Don't be put off by those who seem to be really brilliant players. There are plenty of others that will be at a similar stage to you, and people who join these groups are literally from all over the world. This is social media at its best.

Taking all things into account my conclusion as to whether you are able to learn to play the piano in retirement is that so long as you are clear what your aims are it is most definitely possible and achievable.

In retirement I have learnt that there is more than one way to make music on a piano. So choose to play your piano the way that feels right for you, and enjoy playing it. Play the tunes you love, because you will be able to learn them faster than music you don't like. This is your hobby, your time, your retirement, your life. Let your piano bring you joy.

Near the beginning of this book you may remember I told you I have had a love/hate relationship with the piano most of my life.

Not any more though. Since retirement I have come to truly love my piano. I do hope you will love yours also.

Appendix 1

A list of books you may find helpful

Tutor books for adults

There is a whole wealth of books suitable for younger beginners in general and adult beginners in particular, but listed here are those that I believe are the best for those who are beginning or returning to the piano in retirement. However, if you have decided to take lessons from a teacher and you need to get your own books and be guided by what your teacher recommends.

John Thompson Adult Piano Course. This course has been around a long time but is still highly thought of by many. It comes as a series of graded books. These are not the same as the Grades awarded for those who work through the exams set by the Associated Board, or Trinity College, or any of the other exam boards, but for some people they do give the satisfaction of making progress and moving forward.

Alfred's All in One Course – Wilfred Palmer 'Alfred's' is the publisher here, and there are many books produced by Alfred's for all ages and stages of piano learning. This book is quite comprehensive, covering Practical Lesson, Theory and Technique. It is available with a comb binding which is always useful as the book will hold still on the music stand of the piano easily. The book is really designed for someone who is having lessons from a teacher, but looking at the reviews on Amazon, it seems some people have started to teach themselves using this book.

Classic Piano Course by Carol Barrett. This book is also better for a someone who has a teacher. There are some well known tunes which have been arranged to make them simple to learn, and also some original compositions by Carol Barrett herself. This is a series of graded books, so again, you feel you are making progress.

Adult Piano Adventures by Nancy and Randall Faber. There is level one and level two of these books, and they are my personal favourites, both for self teaching and for those who have a teacher. They come with a spiral bound edition, and besides the basic course there are also three other supplementary books to go with each level, not compulsory by any means but nevertheless they are very useful editions to your piano library. These three extra books are Classics, Popular and Christmas Music, and there are some lovely arrangements in all of the books, which will add interest to your playing. Just one thing to be aware of – the Christmas books are a good collection of well known Christmas music, but some of the carols that you might want to play are set to the American tunes, rather than the tunes which are popular in the U.K. This might not be a problem to you, but it is better to be forewarned.

For those retirees who reached Grade 4 or 5 on the piano when they were younger, they should not need to start at the very beginning with a tutor book. Instead either of the following two books may be more suitable for them:

Returning to the piano: a refresher book for adults by Wendy Stevens.

Play it again by Melanie Spanswick.
There are three books in this 'Play it again' series, which make up a very comprehensive course for the adult returner, with or without a teacher.

Classical Themes for All Keyboards
This is a useful book containing fifty best-loved classical themes, and they are arranged in such a way that they can be adapted for keyboards, piano or organ. Chord symbols are given for every piece.

Other books mentioned in the main text for those who want to go it alone:

How to Play the Piano by James Rhodes. This is the book that teaches you how to play one classical piece, the Prelude in C by J. S. Bach, from *'The Well-Tempered Clavier'*, and he claims that if you follow his instructions you will be able to play this piece in six weeks, even if you have never played the piano before. It might just be worth a try!

How to play popular piano in 10 easy lessons by Norman Monath. An excellent book with clear instructions. It gets a bit more complicated further on in the book, and by that time you might find the following two books more helpful. Both these two require you to know the basics, which the Norman Monath book will give you.

The following two books have the same title which is **'How to Play from a Fake Book'**.

The first is by Blake Neely and the second by Michael Esterowitz. I can recommend both of them, as they give clear instructions on varying the use of left hand chords, and using chord inversions to good effect.

If you learn to play from a 'Fake book' there is then a wealth of music written for you in every style you could imagine, from Beatles, to Jazz, to Classical, and much more. You will never be short of new music to learn and enjoy. There is a series of books under the umbrella '**The Ultimate Collection of Fake Books'.** For example, the Classical Fake Book is a collection of over 650 classical themes, the Jazz Fake Book has 625 jazz classics, the Beatles Fake book has 200 of the Beatles best songs. There is also a Country Collection, Popular Songs, Wedding Music to name just a few. They will keep you busy for a long time.

Piano & Keyboard Chords by Jake Jackson. This is an easy to use, spiral bound book, which illustrates one chord on every page, showing the position of the chord for the left hand on the left side of the book, and the position of the same chord for the right hand on the right side of the book. It also gives the correct fingering of each chord for each hand, and all the inversions of every chord. If you are learning piano using the chord method this is an invaluable addition to you library.

Memoirs of a Secret Pianist by Robert M. Fells A short memoir aimed at 'baby boomers', written by an American gentleman who found the joy of returning to the piano in later life.

The Piano Shop on the Left Bank by T.E. Carhart. The author of this charming book is an American living in Paris, intrigued by a piano repair shop hidden away near his apartment. When he is finally allowed inside this hidden world of a Paris atelier, his love affair with the piano is reawakened.

Described as '*Quirky, tender and beguiling*' by the Sunday Telegraph, this book is well worth a read for piano lovers.

Appendix 2

If you are considering buying a digital piano first take a look at: www.ukpianos.co.uk. The owner of this firm, Graham Howard, has provided a free 'Digital Piano Buyer's Guide' which you can download. He has given each piano a 'Howard Score' so you can see which are the best, most reliable, and which particular features each piano offers.

Even if you don't buy from Graham Howard, his guide gives useful information when you visit your local music shop looking for a digital piano.

The ones that normally come top of his list are Yamaha, especially the Arius range, or the more expensive Clavinova. Roland and Cassio are also known to be good and reliable makes.

For a piano dealer try **The Piano Gallery** in Faringdon, near Oxford. They supply quality new and reconditioned acoustic pianos, to suit all pockets. They also do piano removals, repairs, reconditioning, tuning and long and short term hire.

Visit them in person or online, where you can take a virtual tour of the shop. You will find the staff very helpful, and their experienced piano moving removal men will deliver all over the country.

Printed in Great Britain
by Amazon

82118638R00058